CW01657389

We

This book is filled with visual
collaboration and communica...
written for people and teams working within an agile software development context.

The pages within only depict examples. Nothing else. No deep theoretical explanations. No explanation of Agile or Scrum. No references to Gamification. No discussion on how the brain interprets visual input or how our behaviors are influenced by visual information. There are other books written on those topics.

If a page contains an arrow (➡) in the upper corner, it means that there is a link to a blog or an article with more information to be found on the page "More information".

If a page contains a heart (❤) you will find a person or team credited on the page "Sources of inspiration".

The examples in this book might be perceived as if they are the best and only way of doing things. Of course that is not true. The examples are not best practice. They are only suggestions. You need to adapt them to your team's context and needs.

This book is not intended to be read cover to cover. Browse. Jump back and forth. Pick what you like. Combine the ideas whichever way you find useful. Experiment and evaluate. Evolve or throw away.

Have fun!

Content

Introduction

The juicy stuff

Appendixes...

General Advice

Accessible – Position your wall with visualizations in the area where the team sits. You want it easily visible for everyone in the room.

Simple - The wall needs to be easy to update. If you make it too cumbersome to update, the wall will probably deteriorate. If you suspect that it's not up to date, you will stop trusting it. If you don't trust it, you will update it even less frequently.

Clean – If you put love and care into designing the wall you will probably respect it more and want to continue to keep it nice and tidy. Don't go bananas, choose components with care.

Core flows – Design for the normal cases and core flows. Choose additional components based on the behaviors you want to change. Treat exceptions like exceptions.

Evaluate – Your wall is a living thing. Evaluate each component's value and design regularly. Improve, adjust or abandon.

Visualize your workflow

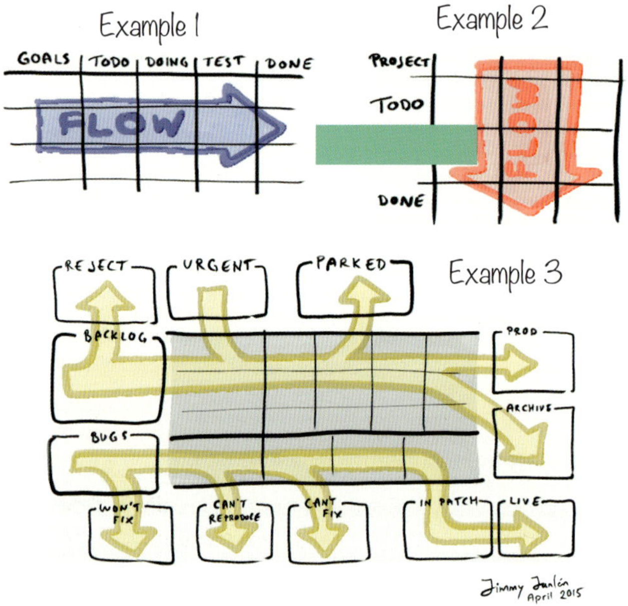

Use boxes, lines, rows and columns to **describe your workflow** and which states work transitions between. Use Post-its to describe the work to be done which flows through your workflow. There is no right or wrong, keep on experimenting until you find a good representation of your workflow, a view that helps you see progress, collaborate, plan, do forecasts, and that reveals bottlenecks.

Tips

Write on Post-its with a **proper pen**, thicker than a normal pencil (like Sharpies, Pilot SignPens or similar). Don't write small text, it needs to be readable from a couple of meters. Only using **CAPS** almost automatically makes the text bigger and more readable.

Buy **proper Post-its**. Avoid the cheap fake ones. Get a lot of different sizes and colors. I can recommend Super Sticky Post-its and Stattys.

To make it simpler to draw straight lines on a whiteboard, get a **big ruler**.

Visualize your policies

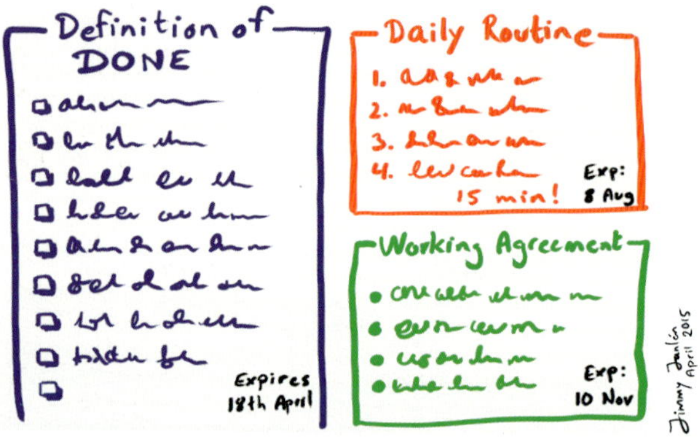

Make your policies, routines, working agreements and rules explicit and visible. Create posters or dedicate a portion of your whiteboard wall to your rules.

Making the policies explicit and visible forces you to come to a shared understanding within the team. It also gives you something concrete to refer to when you're discussing how to improve your way of working. Every policy should also have an **expiration date** (3-6 months into the future). When a policy expires, review it! Make a conscious decision to keep, modify or to abandon it.

Yet another tip is to skip the bottom line and add an empty bullet, signaling that there is more to come.

Avatars

Visualize who is working on which task with the use of **avatars**. If you work on a task, put your avatar on that task. The simplest version is names on small **Post-its**. More elaborate alternatives includes writing the initials on round **magnets**. But way more fun is to have **photos** of the team members. Even though I find it confusing, many teams like characters, such as South Park figures or cartoons. At least, **write the names** so that new team members don't have to guess who is Boba Fett and who is Darth Vader.

Use **Tack-it** or **magnetic tape** to make them stick to the board.

Legend

A good visualization that a team likes and continues to use over time tends to get more and more complex as the team adds more and more information to it.

To make it easy to understand for new team members, and curious colleagues – provide a **legend** that explains the colors, icons and symbols.

Inbox

Are extra tasks frequently added by creative team members? Do you suffer from tasks introduced into the sprint by people/managers outside the team, asking specific team members for help? Does this sabotage the focus on the sprint goals? Add the **Inbox** policy!

Policy: new tasks aren't added to Planned or Doing, they must be placed in the Inbox. The following standup **the whole team decides** if the task should be done or not, i.e. if it's valuable and aligned with the sprint's goal. If the team decides it shouldn't be done now, it goes into the product backlog or into the trash bin.

Each Inbox should be empty by the end of the Daily Stand-up.

2 Avatars - One big, One small

Each team member has **two avatars**, one big printed in color and one small printed in grayscale.

They mark which tasks that team member is currently working on. The big one signals the **main focus**. When blocked on the main task, the smaller grey avatar signals where the person is **helping out**.

Each team member is only allowed these two avatars. If the person wants to start a third task he/she either needs to finish any of the current ones, or put one of the current ones in the parking lot or move back the task from Doing to Planned.

If you currently only have one avatar for each team member, please ignore this example. You are good :-)

Days 'til Demo

Days 'til Demo is a simple **countdown to the next demo**. Its purpose is to raise awareness and to help teams **remember** to plan and prepare for the demo. And of course to raise the **expectations** for everyone else.

It simply shows the number of days left until the demo. The last one reads "TODAY at 2pm" (or something similar).

It's preferably placed in a highly visible place, such as by the coffee machine or next to the toilets. And yes, a manual one like this needs to be manually updated by someone. This could be a good thing since it reminds the team that the day is approaching.

Confidence Smileys

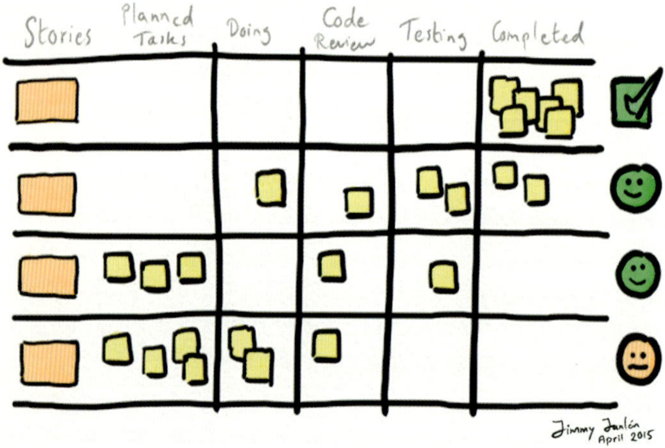

This is a powerful alternative (or complement) to a Sprint Burndown.

At the end of every Daily Stand-up meeting the team asks themselves; **how confident are we that we will be able to finish each User Story by the end of the Sprint**. The answer is represented by a Confidence Smiley.

The team quickly goes through each lane/User Story and updates the color of the **Confidence Smiley**. When in disagreement, the most pessimistic voice wins.

Confidence Smileys (cont)

Happy/Green smiley = We are confident that we will be able to finish this story by the end of this sprint.

Nervous/Orange smiley = We will probably not be able to finish this story.

Sad/Red smiley = No way we will be able to finish this story.

Green checkbox = User story is DONE.

When a smiley shifts (from green to orange, or from orange to red) the team grabs the opportunity to discuss what they need to do, how they can help out, and if they need to alert Product Owners and Stakeholders on changes in the forecast.

Confidence Smileys offer an instant and simple overview of the team's sprint progress for anyone else as well.

Lane priority

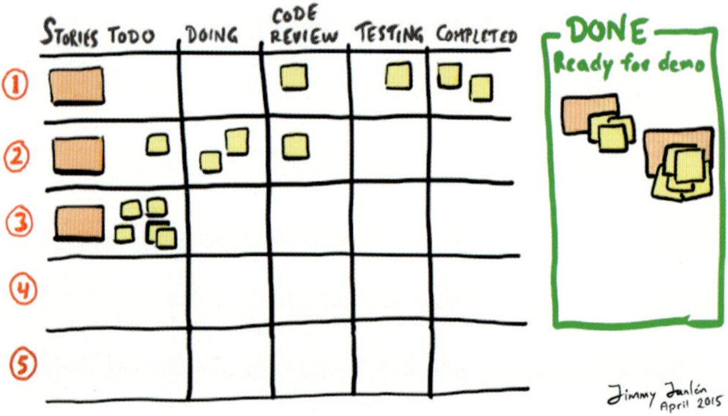

This is more of a process/working agreement tip than a visualization tip.

In order to work more efficiently as a team and to collaborate more on finishing stories rather than starting new ones – **agree to help out working on stories together in priority order**. Place the story of highest priority on the top, then rank the rest according to priority.

When a story has finished, move it to the "DONE / Ready for Demo" area. This will leave an empty lane. Some teams move all other Post-its up one lane to fill the gap.

Blocker Notes

If you for some reason become blocked while working on a task, preventing you from moving forward - add a **red blocker note** on top of that task. This makes the reason known for everyone, and also works as a follow-up reminder.

Review the blockers during the Daily Stand-up and discuss how to **address and resolve** each of them.

The **description clearly states why** you are blocked, who you are waiting for (and why), or what the problem is. To make it even clearer, write your own name and the date you became blocked in the corner of the Post-it.

Dependency Spider

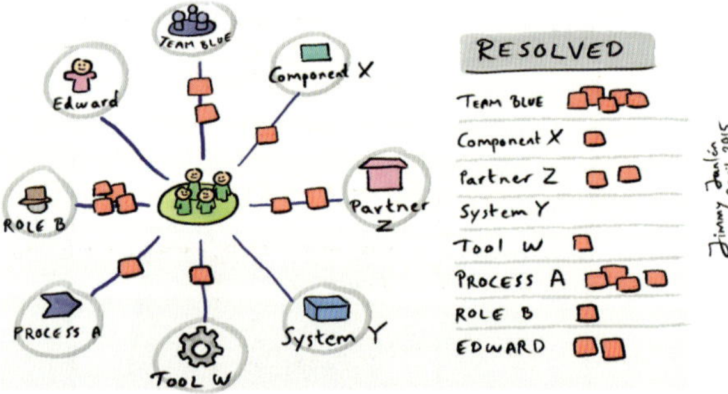

Draw a spider with your team in the middle. Around your team, draw your **dependency sources** that sometimes block your progress or force you to wait for some kind of response. On the legs of the spider you continuously add notes describing how you are currently blocked or dependent on that source.

When resolved, move the ticket to the “Resolved” area. When it’s time for a retrospective, grab Post-its of the most common sources and analyze what you can do to reduce or minimize the pain and frequency of those dependencies. To ensure that you’re not sub-optimizing for your team’s convenience, include the other teams or persons into the discussion.

A great tool for cross-company (and release train) retrospectives as well.

Dotting

Every day, put a new **dot** on each task in progress. Put a dot regardless if someone is actively working on it or not. When everything is running smoothly (given that the tasks are broken down enough) no single task should get more than a few dots. If the dots starts building up, you know that something is wrong and that you need to talk about it.

Dotting is a simple and powerful way of revealing problems and bottlenecks. The same principle can be applied for other columns, such as "Waiting for code review", but instead of dots draw a line or use a different color for the dots.

Absence Calendar

This calendar shows when people know they will be away and **absent** from the office doing something else, avoiding "Does anyone know where Julie is today?" moments.

Each team member writes his/her name on the date(s) **when they know in advance they will be off** on vacation, attending a course or doing something else. The calendar could also include holidays or other important events.

The yellow arrow points to the current day and is moved before the Daily Stand-up meeting.

Days blocked (wasted)

When using Post-it notes to indicate blocked status it can be helpful to keep track of the days since the blocker was introduced.

On the Daily Stand-up meeting, simply **put a dash on the blocker** note, also known as tally marks. The dashing in itself will remind you and your team to act on the impediment or dependency. And the number of dashes will tell you how many days have been wasted waiting for something or someone.

A large number of dashes is an invitation to a serious discussion. Why does the team fail to resolve its impediments? Do they lack support? Motivation?

Due dates and boxes

Sometimes there is a strict due date on fixing things, like a bug for a critical patch. To visualize this, write the date of the **deadline** the task has to be finished by, and **draw one box for each day that remains until that date**.

On the Daily Stand-up meeting, cross one of the boxes. This way you can easily see when time is running out and how many days are left.

Sometimes the bug needs to be dealt with right away forcing you to drop whatever else you are doing. But sometimes there is some leeway, allowing you to wrap things up before addressing the semi-urgent task. That's when due dates and boxes comes in handy.

Question icon

Sometimes you have a question about something, but the right team member isn't around, and it's possible to wait until the team's next Daily Stand-up meeting. If that's the case, you mark the task you have a question about with a **Question icon**.

During the Daily Stand-up meeting the team makes sure to scan the wall for Question icons, addressing them and removing them one by one.

Urgent lane + policy

Not everything can be planned and foreseen during the sprint planning. To deal with urgent unplanned tasks in a structured and transparent way, add an **URGENT lane**.

Since urgent tasks are never planned, the "Planned" (Tasks Todo) column isn't needed. Use that area instead to clearly state the **policy that describes what counts as an urgent task**. Which criteria need to be fulfilled for a task to be allowed to go straight into the urgent lane? If the criteria are not met, the task should be considered during the next sprint planning or the next Backlog Grooming session..

The urgent lane should normally be empty! Remember that every time you introduce something into that lane you create waste in terms of task switching and multitasking. With great powers come great responsibility. Don't abuse the urgent lane.

Bomb icon ♥

One team I worked with decided to get rid of the Urgent Lane. It was misused, always cramped with "important" tasks and sabotaged the team's ability to focus and plan.

Since all tasks were now related to a story there was no way for an urgent task to enter the wall until a lane on the Kanban board was empty. This worried the Product Owner. So, the Product Owner was given one (one!) **Bomb icon**. He could put that on any task he wanted. Anyone who could help out paused whatever they were doing and worked on that task instead until it was done.

(The Bomb icon was used less and less frequently since the pain and cost of adding it to the wall quickly became apparent.)

Parking Lot

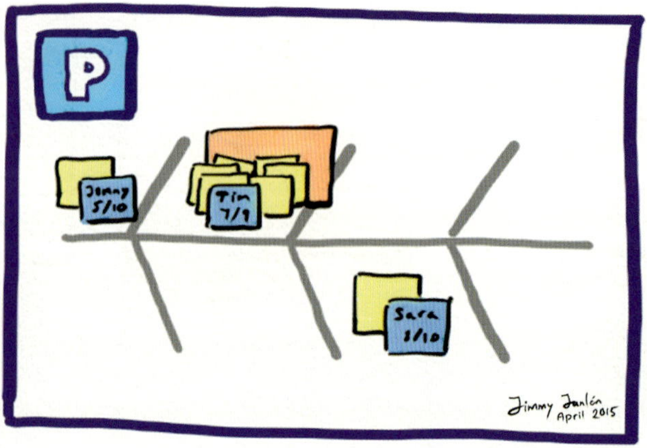

If the team has temporarily stopped working on a story (or paused a specific task) due to changes in priority – make that clear and transparent by moving the Post-its to a **Parking Lot** area.

Moving the story/task away from the primary board also reduces the chance that people accidently work on a paused task (i.e. increased unnecessary multitasking).

When a story or task becomes parked, write a **Parking Ticket** with the **date** when it became parked and **who** was working on it.

Achievement Posters

At the end of every sprint (or every second week if you use Kanban) summarize your **team's achievements**. To build pride and celebrate accomplishments is as important as planning ahead and focusing on the next challenge.

Set a timer on fifteen minutes during which you help out to remember and summarize. The prouder you are over an accomplishment, the bigger the Post-it. Use different colors for different kinds of events. Once the poster is hung on the wall, applaud yourselves.

Kaizen board

To ensure that the actions decided upon during the retrospective are followed through, write down the actions on Post-its and bring them to the wall.

If the Post-its do not have a natural fit on your normal board, create a small separate **Retrospective Actions** Kanban board (sometimes known as a **Kaizen Board**) where you can track the improvement work.

If you use Avatars, use them same the way as you use them for the regular wall.

Team Members with Hats ♥

Make it easy for your colleagues to know who is who in your team with the use of a **Team Members Catalog**. Also, visualize who is having which role with the use of **hat icons**. If you want you can add their primary skill, email address or some other additional information.

Team Habits ♥

During a retrospective it's quite common that you decide to try to implement some new habits, to do something differently from now on. If you have a Working Agreement, it should probably be updated. If you don't have a working agreement (or don't feel the new policy fits there) create a **Team Habits** area on your wall.

Newly decided habits that you have agreed to try to follow are written down on orange Post-its. Once they have become true habits, re-write them on green Post-its. If you become sloppy, change it back to orange. Review your habits on a regular basis (for example once a month).

Rotating facilitator's hat ♥

Does the Scrum Master really need to be the facilitator of every Daily Stand-up? Of course not. Why not **rotate the facilitation**.

Facilitating a good, short and concrete Daily Stand-up meeting is difficult. By rotating the facilitation you share the experience and more people get to practice facilitation skills.

To emphasize the rotation of the facilitator, get a nice **hat** for the facilitator to wear.

Interruption buckets

Do you suspect that most of your interruptions have a common origin and source? Do you have a growing frustration towards someone or something? To turn that frustration into a data driven insight and data driven decision to change something, **collect your interruptions on Post-its and sort them according to category**.

Do this for a couple of weeks and then bring the notes to a workshop where you analyze and discuss how you can reduce the frequency or pain of the interruptions. Or, instead of having a time-limit, **whenever there are 5 or more notes in a bucket – call for an interruption reduction workshop**.

Daily Stand-up timer

One team I was working with repeatedly decided that they should really limit the Daily Stand-up meeting to 15 minutes, but never succeeded to accomplish it. One day I placed my tablet on a small table (that happened to be positioned in front of the wall) and started a **timer**. I didn't explain why.

That simple thing made everyone slightly more focused and avoided a lot of detail derailing. And voilà! As if the tablet held a secret superpower, the Daily Stand-up meetings most of the times finished well below 15 minutes.

Note: The goal of the Daily Stand-up meeting is of course not to finish within 15 minutes, it is to figure out how we as a team need to collaborate today to accomplish our goals.

Stand-ups on time + high score

Do you think you are getting better at starting your Daily Stand-ups on time? Why not measure it?

Every day you start the Daily Stand-up on time, increase your "Daily started on time"-score. If you start it late, reset it to zero. Next to the **counter**, write your **high-score** so far. If you can, think of a fun reward for the team every time you break your own record.

Other examples of counter and high scores (aka "**chains**") are "We fixed more bugs today than were reported", "Days with zero bug reports", and "Urgent lane empty by the end of the day".

Parking lot with states

When you pause a full story and move the associated tickets to a **Parking Lot** it might be a good idea to **preserve the states of the tasks**.

This takes more space, but that could be used as a WIP-limit, i.e. no more than one story may be paused at any single point in time.

Don't forget to write down the date when the story became paused.

This approach can be useful when something urgent arrives mid-sprint temporarily overriding the priorities.

Progress Pie ♥

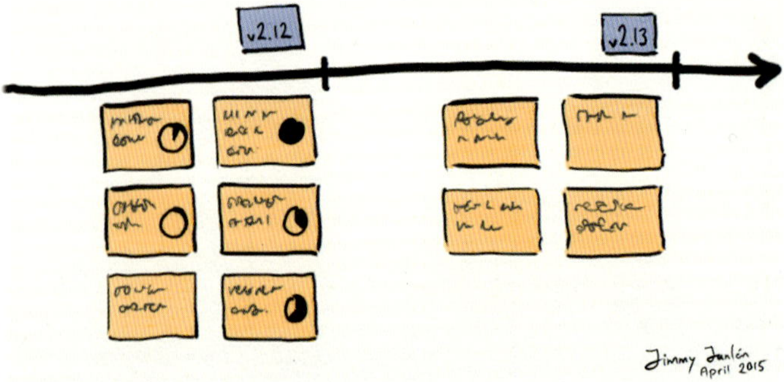

Do you have your roadmap visualized on your wall and would like to visualize progress of Epics related to a specific release? Some rough estimate is usually enough, for example a **progress pie**.

Draw a circle on the Post-it and ask "How much is done?". Fill in the pie according to the answer. An empty circle would mean "not begun". A full circle "Ready to ship".

This of course triggers discussions about what is needed for a full circle, which is a good thing! When needed: clarify acceptance criteria and maybe replace the Epic with sliced User Stories.

Box on the floor

Are you standing so far from the wall that you can't read the Post-its? Do people have to walk across the room to move a Post-it? Does it look like people are afraid of the wall?

Try **Drawing a box on the floor** (using white adhesive tape) in front of the team's board.

I've found that for some strange reason, people like to stand inside boxes. Don't be surprised if this simple trick makes people stand closer to the board. At least, you don't have anything to lose by trying it once.

Adhesive tape doesn't stick that well to the floor, but I would not recommend painting or drawing directly on the floor.

After Party

When people derail in detailed discussions during the Daily Stand-up meeting, pause them and add the topic to **"Immediately after"**. The policy could be that whenever anyone makes a T-shaped hand signal, the discussion is moved to after the Daily Stand-up.

Once the Daily Stand-up is wrapped up, those that need to (and those that want to) stick around and discuss the listed topics. Some people call this the **"After party"**.

As each topic is resolved, cross it over. When all have been discussed, clean the area so that it's ready for the next Daily Stand-up.

For some teams this is a great approach to make the Daily Stand-up meetings shorter and more concrete.

Team Rhythm/Cycle

Many teams who Kanban still experience value from having a **rhythm**. For example, backlog grooming every week, demo and retrospective every second week, and so on.

Visualizing this rhythm, and **where in the cycle the team is**, helps focus and provides a sense of structure to an otherwise response and pull driven work environment.

The cycle can be visualized in many ways: a clock (example A), a road (B), a game board (C). Pick whatever you like and find amusing.

Improvement Lane

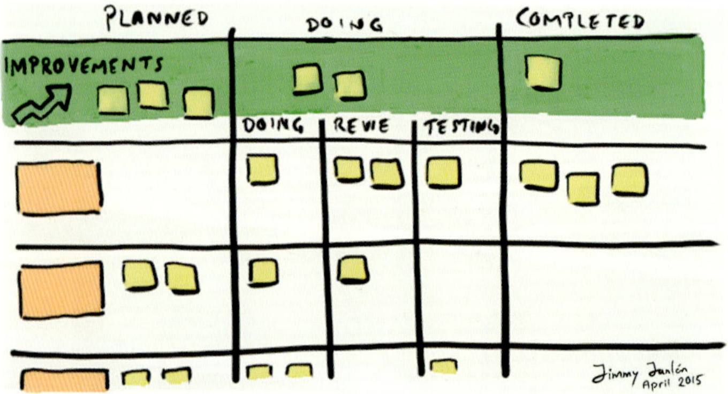

To make your retrospective improvement actions a natural part of your planning and Daily Stand-ups, add an **Improvement Lane** to the board.

Some teams place the Improvement lane at the bottom and have the policy that if you're blocked on your primary work you work on improvements until you become unblocked, or someone else needs help.

Other teams place the lane on top, signaling that the improvement actions are the most important thing to finish first (right after urgent production problems).

Today's Headlines

Many times teams start or end their Daily Stand-up with a general information sharing moment.

To reduce the chance that you forget to share something important with your team, add your news headlines to the **"Today's Headline"** whiteboard area as soon as you come to think of a topic.

When the news or information has been shared, clear the area so that new headlines can be added for the next day.

Late = Cake

Draw a circle. Slice it up in 8 slices. This represents a cake. **When someone arrives late to the Daily Stand-up write that person's name in one of the slices.**

When the cake circle is full, count the "winner". The winner bakes a cake that the team enjoy the next day.

An alternative for this is to write a list of the team members. When someone is late, he or she gets a tick. Three or more ticks mean cake.

If you don't like cake, or this policy makes the team fat, try another policy.

Task size < 1 day

When tasking (i.e. breaking down the work that needs to be performed to complete a User Story) **don't stop splitting the tasks until each task can be completed within a day**.

This policy makes it easier to see progress and bottlenecks. It also triggers deeper collaborative discussions during the planning sessions.

Furthermore, if you use Dotting, you know there is something fishy going on if a task starts collecting dots since no single task should have more than one dot.

If you use a Sprint Burndown, you can instead of summarizing hours summarize the number of tasks. Much faster!

Task describes result

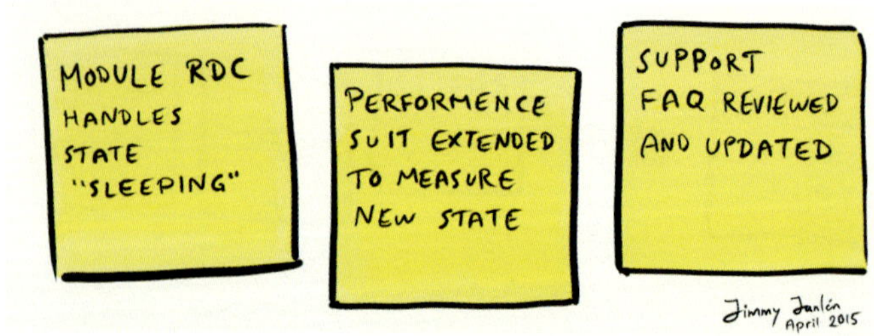

The texts on the Post-its matter. Spending a couple of extra seconds to describe the work a Post-it refers to can make a huge difference.

Don't simply write a keyword or a vague description of the work – describe what state we are in when the task has been completed. Another way to phrase the same thing: **don't describe the work, describe the result**.

When applying this policy, it becomes much clearer for the team what the goal of the task is and what's expected.

Portable boards

It's quite common that planning or retrospective meetings take place in meeting rooms from where the team's physical board isn't visible. And it's also quite common that you would like to bring part of the wall to those meetings.

One solution to this is to create portable boards, i.e. boards that you can lift down from the wall and bring with you. For example, there are small whiteboards you hang on the wall as you hang a painting. You could also create a **foldable mini-board from foam boards** and then attach some hooks to it.

Flowglass

Do you want to signal to your colleagues that you want some undisturbed time to focus on something difficult? Reaching a mental state of flow usually requires some undisturbed time, especially when working with complex work such as software engineering.

Invest in an hourglass. **Whenever you require some undisturbed flow time, turn the hourglass over and put it on your table**. For clarity, perhaps add a note next to it. Your friends can now see that you actively request some time to focus. It's also easy for them to roughly estimate when it's ok to come back to you (based on the amount of sand left).

Kudo Wall ♥

Show more love in the team! Whenever you feel someone else did something great that deserves appreciation and recognition, write a Kudo card and put in on the team's **Kudos Wall**!

A Kudo wall is a great way to nurture intrinsic motivation within a team and to self-reward good behaviors.

You can use Post-its, design your own cards that you print, or buy them online here:
https://management30.com/product/kudo-cards/

Task Progress Bar

Some tasks get stuck on the wall because they either describe a big chunk of work, or the amount of work turned out to be more than first anticipated. When that happens draw a **progress bar** (on the task Post-it) which is updated during the Daily Stand-up.

If you use dotting (see example "Dotting") as a habit you could add the policy: as soon as a task gets two or more dots, we add a progress bar and discuss what is needed to complete the task.

Awesome Person Dice

Just for fun, choose today's **Awesome Person of the Day** by rolling a dice at the beginning of the Daily Stand-up meeting.

Each side of the dice has a team member's name written on it. Are you more than six people in the team, no worries – there are 8 and 10 sided dice as well.

Once a Today's Awesome Person has been selected, applaud that person and put their photo in the Today's Awesome Person photo frame that hangs on the wall.

Why? Because it's fun.

Story Point Ruler

To get better at doing relative Story Point estimation as a team, create a **Story Point Ruler**.

By the end of every sprint (for example during the Sprint Review meeting) ask yourselves, for every story completed: In hindsight, given what we know now - how many Story Points should this user story have been? Put the User Story on that place on the ruler.

When it's time to estimate new stories (with for example Poker Planning), simply compare that story to the stories already estimated on the ruler. As time goes by, clean the ruler so that it doesn't become too crowded. Keep the good examples and remove similar User Stories.

Reward Jar

Creating new habits can be difficult. To reward yourselves for your efforts of converting new policies to habits, get a **Reward Jar**. List the things you want to reward yourselves for (together as a team), including the score for each achievement. Agree on some milestones that are put on the jar.

Whenever you "score", place a marble in the jar. When you hit a milestone: collect the reward!

Release Credits

By the end of every movie, there are release credits acknowledging everyone involved in creating the masterpiece. Why would you deserve any less!? Celebrate your achievement of finishing a sprint with the creation of a **Release Credits** poster.

I've seen teams who have chosen themes such as space missions, superhero movies, rock bands etc. Whatever makes you tick. The responsibility to create the poster could rotate, or you create it as a team during the Sprint Review.

Task Estimation Boxes

One simple approach to learn if things take longer than expected is to **estimate the work for a task with boxes**. Two boxes could for example mean a full day's work.

During the Daily Stand-up you cross the boxes as you work on the task. Continue to cross even when there are no more boxes. This technique will make it easy to see when something turned out to be harder than initially estimated, which in turn should trigger a discussion on how to help out.

The estimation could take place during the sprint planning or when the task is moved from "Planned" to "Doing".

WIP Limits

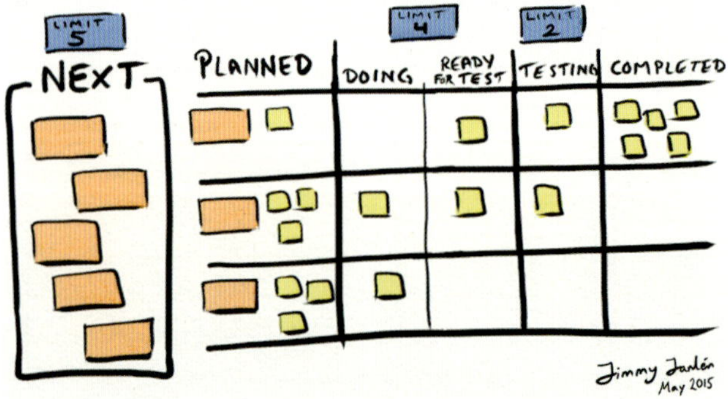

In the example above the team has a **limited Work In Progress** (WIP) in several dimensions. They only work on a maximum of three stories at any given time. If they want to start a fourth, they first need to finish any of the ongoing. If "Doing" + "Ready for Test" are full (joint limit of 4) they aren't allowed to start on a fifth task. They first need to help out testing, moving tasks down the board. And so on.

Put the WIP Limits on Post-its since you probably will change them over time as you try to find a good balance.

Limiting WIP is at the core of Lean and something many successful teams do. Explaining Lean, or why limiting WIP is a great idea, is beyond the scope of this book.

Color according to skill

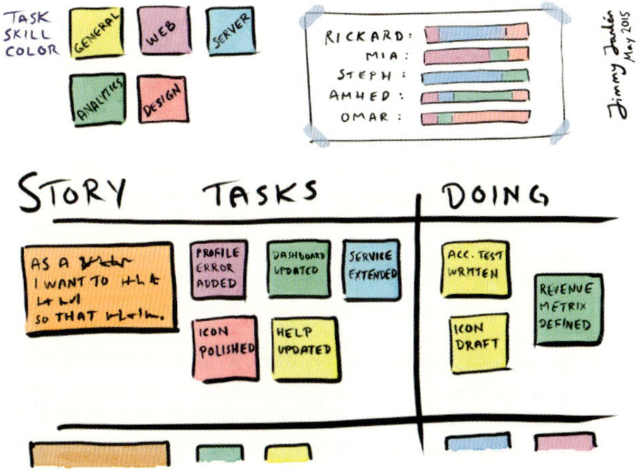

Some teams like to **color the tasks according to the primary skill needed**. During the planning session this helps the team to split work into tasks and to clarify the diversity of work.

I've seen that some teams have a color for testing activities, others have a column named "Testing". You need to experiment to find what works for you.

But, if this technique undermines teamwork - stop using it! Not finding a task with "your" color is no excuse to not collaborate and help out.

Parked by Person

Some teams I've met (who have a **Parking Lot**) make clear who was working on the task when it became paused by **sorting the Post-its by team member**.

When a task becomes paused, the Post-it gets moved to that person's line in the Parking Lot area. When that person, or someone else, picks up the task again it gets moved back to the it's original position on the wall.

Pair Programming Matrix ♥

Are you trying to do more pair programming in your team? Would you like to visualize how much you pair during a week? Try putting up a **Pair Programming Matrix**.

Whenever you've done a pairing session, make a tick in the corresponding box. You need to agree as a team how much pairing is required for a tick.

Set a date when you review and talk about the results. If you want to continue tracking your pairing, reset the matrix and agree upon a new review date.

Daily Stand-up Routine

Instead of just jumping into doing the Scrum default "round", **make the routine of the Daily Stand-up a conscious design** by writing it down. Once written down it becomes easier to have constructive discussions on how to improve it.

It also makes it easier to rotate the responsibility of facilitating the Daily Stand-up.

The same approach could also of course be applied to other kinds of meetings such as Sprint Planning, Backlog Grooming, Sprint Review, etc.

Pause Icon

Sometimes you need to pause work on a task because another thing has become more urgent. You're not necessarily blocked by anything, but you are nonetheless not working on it at the moment.

In order to make that clear and transparent, put a **Pause Icon** on top of that task. And for extra clarity you might want to leave your avatar on the task to signal that you were the one working on it.

Another approach to address the same issue is to use a **Parking Lot** instead.

Stress Level Meter ♥

Are there days when you as a team is swamped and stressed with work and just want to be left alone? While other days are calm, almost boring.

To share your stress level with others, making them aware of your mood, put up a **Stress Level Meter** next to the entrance to your team area. Perhaps you have a suitable door frame, a glass wall or something else colleagues need to pass by in order to enter the team area.

At any given point, anyone in the team can move the arrow of the Stress Level Meter, reflecting the mood of the room advising people how to approach the team.

Improvement Theme

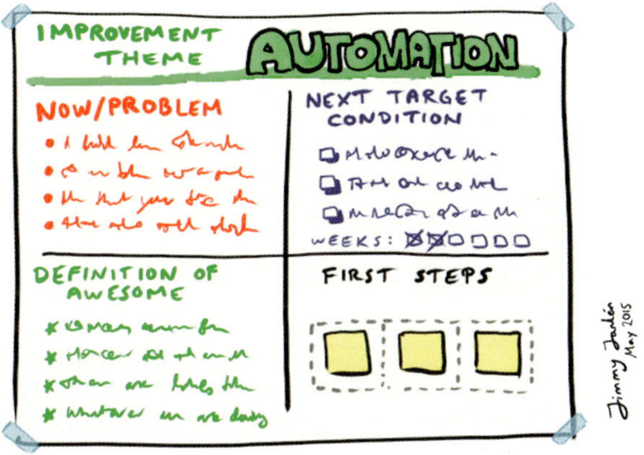

Improvement Theme is a tool in the form of a poster that works as a conveyor belt for continuous improvements once the Retrospective is over. Describe the current situation in the red section. Then define how the situation would look like if it was awesome in the green section. Then ask yourselves, six weeks from now; what realistic and concrete goals can we set that will bring us closer to our "Definition of Awesome?" Then identify the first three smallest steps you can take to get closer to these goals.

Follow up on the steps during the Daily Stand-up and add new ones as tasks are completed. When the six weeks have passed, evaluate the poster and create a new "Next Target Condition".

Test Server Icons & Info

If your team uses several different physical or virtual test environments, and this causes confusion, make it easier to see where things can be tested and the state of each test environment.

When something is ready for testing in a specific test environment, mark the task with the appropriate icon.

Additional details, such as server name, purpose, version, branch, date of upgrade etc., are put somewhere next to the wall. The color of the icons corresponds to the colors of these server notes.

Ready for demo

Teams that Kanban should also of course demo as well. If your team hasn't scheduled a recurring demo, perhaps a **Ready for demo** area can help.

Once a story is done and ready for demo, move it to an empty slot in the first row. When the first row is full, an invitation for a demo is sent out. When the demo is held, all ready-for-demo stories are shown, after which the area is cleared.

Note: This example has been mentioned earlier (see Lane Priority), but is presented here in more detail.

Team Mood Barometer

Team Mood Barometer is a board with a rope on which you position your clothespin with your name. The position of your clothespin reflects your current mood.

You update it whenever you want to. Once a week or maybe several times a day.

If you as a team want to be better at sharing your mood, and how you are feeling, this could be a simple tool to trigger dialog. If someone is far down, you probably want to know if there is something you can do to help that person. It also provides some kind of overview how the team in general is feeling.

Newsletter

In a team all kind of exciting stuff happens. One way to create transparency within the organization (apart from Demos, Townhall meetings, Community of Practices, etc.) is to send newsletters from the team.

As interesting things happen, add a bullet to the **Newsletter** content list. Write a paragraph about it in the shared document. When you have six news items to share, convert the document into an email and send to your colleagues. Writing the newsletter could be a rotating responsibility. The person who is supposed to write the next newsletter has his or her avatar next to the list.

Out of Office

I've seen some teams dedicate a small area of the team wall to show where people are if they are not at the office.

As soon as someone learns that a person is sick, working offsite (conference, course, etc.), on vacation, or home doing VAB, the person's avatar is moved to the corresponding slot.

Additional information can of course be added on Post-its, for example: when will the person be back from vacation.

Note: VAB is perhaps very Swedish... it means "Getting paid for staying at home taking care of my sick kid".

Exploratory Testing Wheel

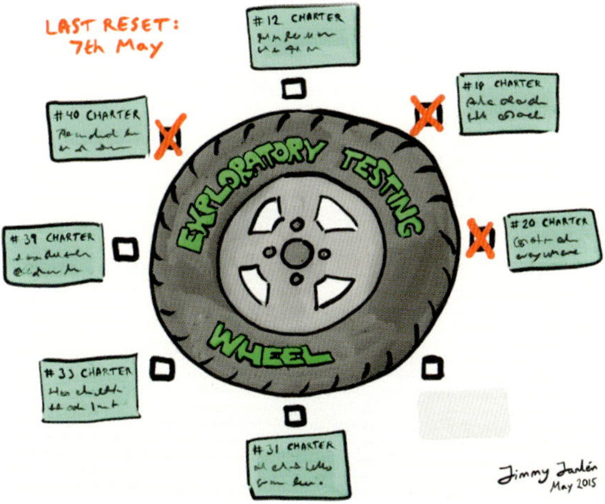

If you vacuum a huge floor with an automatic semi-dumb vacuum robot, at least at some point in time every area of the floor has been vacuumed. You could use the same approach to testing.

Choose a couple of Exploratory Test Charters. Place them around a wheel. Make it a policy that each member runs one of those charters each week. When done, the charter Post-it is put back on the wheel and the checkbox is crossed. When the wheel is done, replace some of the charters and restart the wheel.

Envelope Collectors

Envelopes are great for collecting Post-it. I've seen teams use them simply for storage, a place to store Post-its instead of throwing them in the bin.

A little more elaborate approach is to put up new envelopes every month and then **store different Post-its in different collectors**. At the end of the month the finished stories and tasks are summarized and analyzed. What was the ratio of value adding (User Stories) work vs bug fixing? Planned vs unplanned work? Most common source of interruptions? Common causes of Urgent tasks?

If you are nostalgic you can put the envelopes in a plastic pocket, label it with a date and put it in a binder.

Limit by Space

If your team does Kanban or some version of Scrumban and have a hard time honoring the WIP Limits you have set for yourselves, perhaps this approach can help you.

Instead of writing the WIP Limits, adjust the spaces. Make the boxes and areas containing the Post-its so small that **you can't physically fit more Post-its than the space allows without breaking the WIP Limit**.

This approach also makes it bluntly obvious if the WIP Limit has been broken somewhere, just look for Post-its stacked upon each other.

Retro Input Inbox

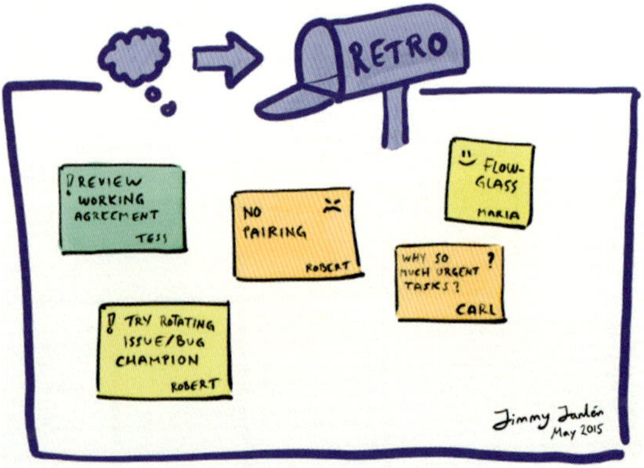

When it's time for the Sprint Retrospective, do you often have a hard time remembering the sprint and what it was you wanted to bring up in the meeting? Why wait to write down your thoughts and ideas until the retrospective, do it continuously!

As soon as something happens or when a thought pops into your mind, capture it, write it down and put it in the "**Retro Input Inbox**" area. If you think it will add value, note the date and author of the note as well.

When it is time for the retrospective, simply bring all the Post-its from the area.

Sprint Info

While doing the sprint planning, why not capture the details of the sprint on the wall. I've seen many teams having really creative **Sprint Information** areas.

Apart from the ID (or number) of the sprint, it could state the sprint's goal. Some teams also name their sprint according to themes (NASA missions, rock stars, super heroes etc.) And then of course you can add a start and an end date, number of people in the team this sprint, date of demo, and so on.

Review Queue

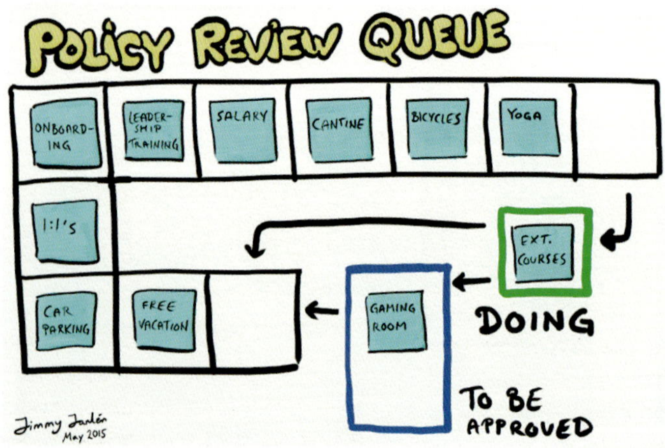

One HR team I was working with had a long list of wiki pages describing different policies and guidelines. They suspected a lot of them needed to be revisited and updated. So, we created a **Policy Review Queue**. Every week one policy was reviewed and updated. Some updates needed approval from someone else so they went through a "To be approved" box. Once done, the ticket moved to the end of the queue. The order and content of the queue was rearranged when needed.

The same approach could of course be applied to technical documentation, website content, FAQs, manuals, etc.

Team Presence Hours ♥

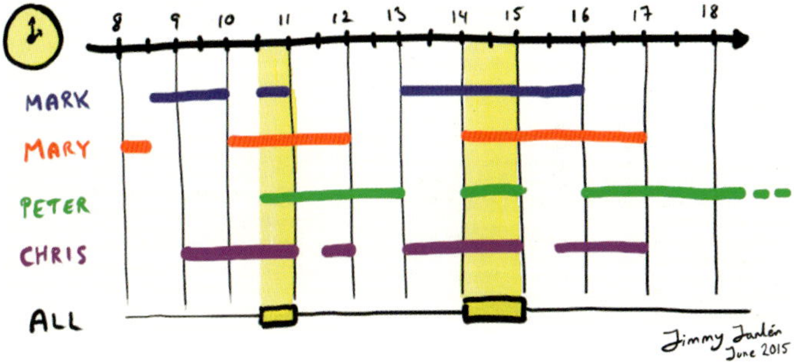

Do you have the feeling that, although you as a team are sitting in the same room, you have trouble getting the communication and collaboration flowing? The reason could be that although you sit together you are not actually all there at the same time during the day.

To explore this, **paint a graph where each person plots when he/she typically arrives**, is away for lunch and is off to recurring meetings. Or even better, record actual data over a two week period. This might reveal opportunities to reschedule some meetings, or others might consider arriving earlier or later.

If the team is **dis-located**, people might even be spread out across different time zones, then this can be very useful and valuable to map out.

Stuff Collectors

Having a hard time finding the right colored Post-its? Do the pens seem to constantly disappear? Why not put up boxes beneath or beside the whiteboard where you can collect them.

You can even add labels that at the same time will function as a legend, explaining the colors of the Post-its.

The boxes could be made out of cardboard and put up using adhesive tape. Or buy yourself shower storage baskets with suction cups, attaching them to the whiteboard itself or a nearby window.

Fail Wall

Do you as a team want to create a safer environment for experimentation and learnings? Perhaps one way to shape your behavior in that direction could be to defuse the drama of failures, and instead celebrate them.

The rules of a **"Fail Wall"** is simple. Whenever you screw up or make a blunder, you describe what happened on a Post-it. You put it up on the Fail Wall and do a failure bow. Here, the other team members should applaud you for sharing something that probably presented a learning opportunity.

You are of course not allowed to put up Post-its on behalf of others.

Pyramid Backlog ♥

Instead of ordering the User Stories of your backlog in a strict order, try sorting them in a **Pyramid Backlog**. In the Backlog Pyramid, there can only be one top priority story. But as you go further down the pyramid, you allow yourselves more and more stories on the same priority level. Whenever the top one slot gets empty (i.e. the team has pulled it into their work) the rest of the stories "bubble" up the pyramid.

You can also impose rules on estimates. For example; stories at priority level three or higher need to be smaller than 8 points. For a story to climb to priority level 5 or above, it needs to have an estimated size. And so on.

Tube Poll

Dropping balls in tubes is a fun way to visualize data. The tubes can be labeled. The colors of the balls could be used to have different meaning.

The possibilities are of course endless, but here are some examples:

- Statistics: Where do bugs originate from? Once a bug has been fixed, drop a ball in corresponding tube.
- Data: Each tube is a sprint. Each ball a Story Point.
- Poll: Each tube represents a question. Green balls for yes, red balls for no.
- Vote: "Refactor" - what class should be the target for the next hack attack?

Promiscuous Map ♥

This visualization is a way of tracking how often pairing happens, and who pairs with whom. It addresses the same behavior as the Pair Programming Matrix.

Whenever you've paired with someone, draw a line between yourself and that other person in the **Promiscuous Map**.

After a couple of days, patterns will probably emerge. How much do we actually pair? Who pairs with whom? Do we want to consciously break some patterns and be better at pairing with different people?

Team Time Zone Clocks ♥

Do you collaborate a lot with teams located in another office, in another time zone?

Having **clocks on the wall** showing the current time at the different offices is a classic way of making it easy to know the time for the different teams.

Another approach could be to put a poster behind your own clock on which you show what time of day it is at the other offices. From a quick glance you know if your far-away-friend is at work, still hasn't arrived or is done for the day.

Activity Dice

When you start your Daily Stand-up, roll the **Team Activity Dice**. The dice will tell you what you should do together as a team today.

It could be having a joint lunch, clean up the team area and make it nicer, make a surprise visit to another team, go outside for a walk, organize a Rock-Paper-Scissor team battle tournament, do 100 push-ups together, make a new dice, afternoon break with ice cream, meditate together for 10 minutes, draw and discuss a Jimmy Card, delete old and obsolete bugs in your digital planning tool, or anything else you fancy doing as a team.

Race Track ♥

Instead of punishing late-comers to the Daily Stand-up, why not reward those that are on time by allowing them to move their figure one step forward on the **race track**? The person that has come the furthest on the race track by the end of the sprint wins an applaud and a group hug. A race like this could also focus on other behaviors and actions, such as...

- Resolving blockers
- Getting committed code reviewed
- Executing retrospective actions
- Finishing tasks
- Reviewing code

Either the winner chooses the rules of the next race, or the team decides this together during the Sprint Planning.

Pre-printed DONE checklists

A simple way of making it easy to remember the agreed upon Definition of DONE is to **print cheat checklists**. Put them in a box or hang them on a nail.

When you start working on a new User Story, grab one of the pre-printed Definition of DONE checklist. As your work progress, you **tick the boxes**.

Tip: Don't print too big batches. The Definition of DONE has a tendency to change a lot over time.

Visualize internal queues

One of the seven wastes of software development is queues. One approach to reveal bottlenecks within a team is to **visualize internal queues**. This can be done by making it visual when tasks are actually being worked on, or waiting to be worked on.

For example: instead of just having a "Test" column, split the column into **"Ready for test" and "Testing"**, or split "Review" into "Waiting for review" and "Reviewing".

If tasks get congested in any of these internal queues, you've found your bottleneck and can start discussing how to address this as a team.

Today's trick ♥

Why not speed up knowledge sharing within the team, making everyone gradually more efficient with your tools, by sharing "**Today's trick**"?

It could be a shortcut, a nice hidden feature of the IDE and tools you are using, or any hack that simplifies your work.

As soon as you learn something new from reading a blog, watching a YouTube tutorial or from pairing with someone – share it!

Servant Manager Door

I've heard many stories about how managers work with trust and transparency by visualizing which organizational impediments they are currently working on. This visualization is sometimes called "**Management Door**" or "**Servant Leadership Board**".

Even though an autonomous team owns their own process and self-organizes their work, they often find a limit to their area of influence, which requires the support of managers to resolve impediments. Being transparent about which impediments you as a manager are currently addressing, and being honest about which one you're currently *not* focusing on, is a simple and powerful way to build trust.

Hourglass Scrum Wall

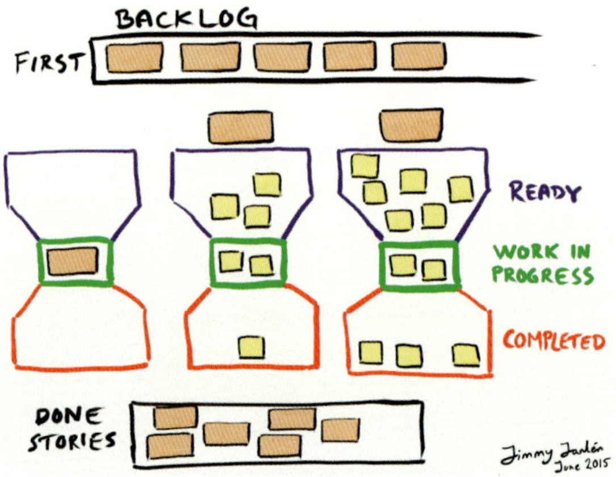

A Scrum wall doesn't need to be in the shape of a grid. The **Hourglass Scrum Wall** replaces a User Story lane with an Hourglass where tasks flow downwards. It provides two natural dimensions for limiting work in progress; the number of concurrent User Stories, and an upper limit of two active tasks per User Story. If a story is too small to be broken down into tasks (i.e. the team can finish the entire story within a day) it simply occupies the whole Hourglass.

Not separating "Work in progress" into "Coding", "Reviewing", and "Testing" and so on also enforces cross-discipline collaboration and knowledge sharing.

Lava Lamps

Nothing beats a visual information radiator that glows. I've seen many teams connecting lava lamps to their Continuous Integration servers, alerting the team when something needs attention. There are several plug-ins for this, and numerous blogs that describe how this can be done.

One team I was working with had two lamps. The red one lit up when the Continuous Integration pipeline encountered a problem (failed to compile, failed test, etc.). The other one lit up when a new high priority bug had been reported.

Arrival/Departure Timeline

I've heard of teams who keep track of important events as their team changes over time. When the team was created, when it got a new name, when its mission changed and **when new team members arrived and when members departed from the team**.

This creates a sense of common history as well as shows how the team has evolved to where it is today. Even other kinds of events could of course be included, such as major releases, game changing decisions and other organizational changes.

I want to learn... ♥

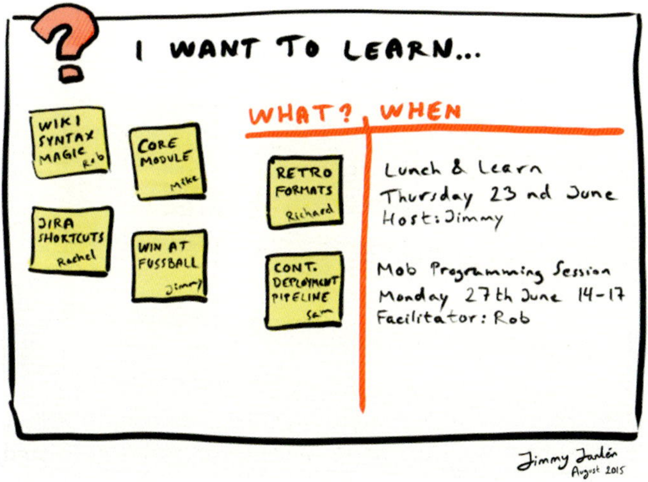

Whenever you feel that you lack knowledge about a tool, want to learn more about some part of the system or wish you were better at something, capture it and put it up on the **"I want to learn..."** poster.

When you spot something that you can contribute with or teach someone else, schedule it and write down when the session, workshop, seminar or lunch & learn will happen. Don't forget to announce it on the Daily Stand-up or any other appropriate meeting.

User Story Flavor Legend

Some teams find it useful to **distinguish between different types of user stories**. Not all prioritized work fit the typical customer value focused User Story template.

Instead of forcing yourselves to write a weird card using User Story format for a patch release or a time boxed investigation or experiment, allow simpler templates when working with non-user centric stories. Make the different flavors of User Stories clear by the use of colors and add the colors to your wall legend.

Color the glass

Does your team have partial glass walls defining your team area, why not put them to use. Glass walls allow you to make really fancy and colorful Scrum or Kanban walls by putting up **colored paper** with adhesive tape **on the other side of the glass**.

You can use different colored papers to emphasize different lanes and areas. You could even use colors to signal status of your work or other important factors.

Concept Cubes

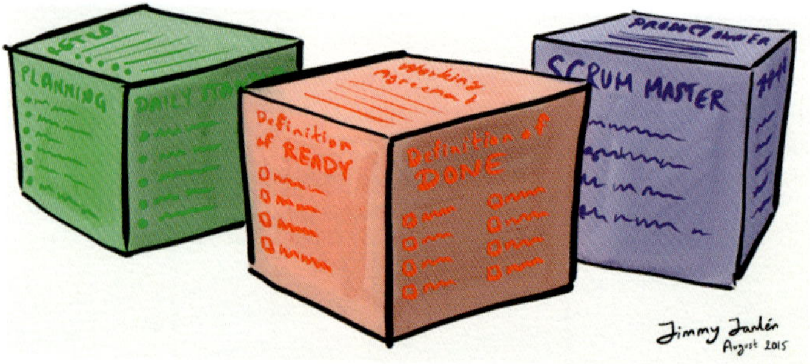

Instead of summarizing the results of a workshop on a poster, or having a working agreements' area on your whiteboard – create a **physical cube**! One side could show the name of the cube and the others contain text and images. A cube invites to curiosity! I've seen people being far more eager to pick up a cube then to stop by and read a poster.

Examples of cubes:

- **Meetings**. Each side describes the purpose and outcome of the different meetings (Daily Stand-up, Planning, Retrospective, etc), as well as the default meeting routine.
- **Working agreements** (Definition of Done, Definition of Ready, Behavior of conduct, Way of working, etc.).
- **Expectations of roles** (Scrum Master, Product Owner, Team member, Development manager, etc.).

Daily Goals

The single most important question to answer during the Daily Stand-up is; what do we need to do today as a team to bring ourselves one step closer to our current goal?

During the Daily Stand-up, if we would define the answer to that question like an achievement we would be proud of – what would that look like? That becomes **the team's goal for that day**.

During the next Daily Stand-up we assess if we accomplished our goal. If we did, we put a happy cross on the note. Then we proceed to define a new goal for today. Always define a new Daily Goal. Don't simply copy yesterday's goal in the case we didn't fulfill it. Everyday is a new day and there is always some circumstance that has changed.

Opportunities by Persona

Instead of having a backlog of User Stories, I've seen teams having **backlogs of opportunities categorized by persona**. The opportunity backlogs feed into the roadmap and into the team's User Story Backlog.

An opportunity is described by:

- **What problem** are we trying to solve? Which need are we exploiting? (Why should we do this?)
- **For whom** are we trying to solve this problem? (Persona)
- **Success criteria**. How will we know that we have succeeded?

Time Invested ♥

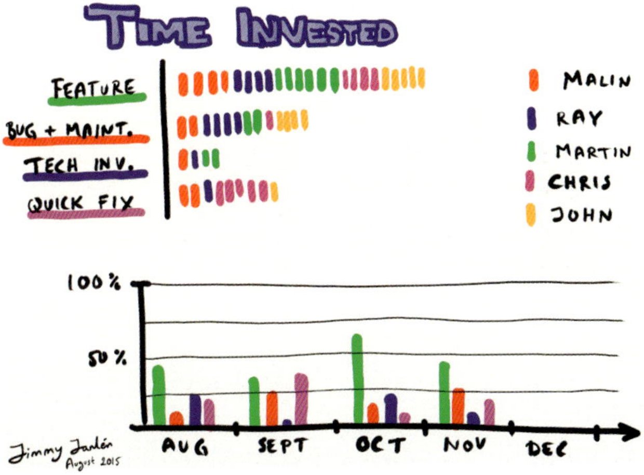

Would you like a lightweight approach for **presenting to your stakeholders how you have been investing your time**?

At the end of every week, sprint or month, roughly estimate how you have spent your time. Each member draws ten bars. Each bar represents 10% of the invested time. The time is distributed into categories such as; feature development, bug fixes and maintenance, technical investment and quick/panic fixes.

The historical summary is then communicated to stakeholders.

Release Train Departures

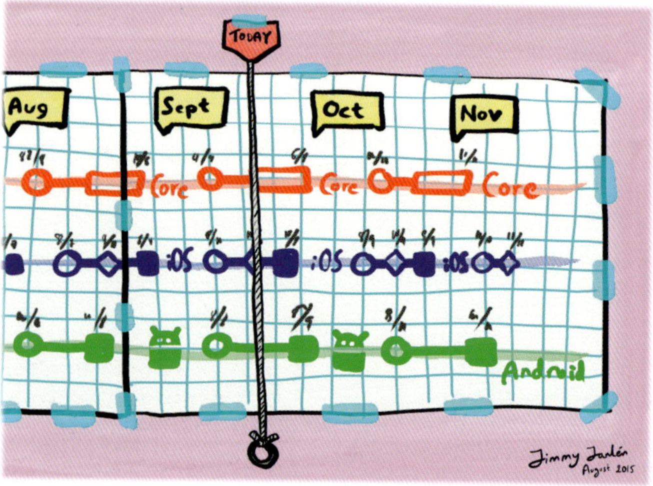

If your team have to plan your work according to release train departures, why not visualize the different release trains and **each release train's upcoming departures**. Each "row" shows the events for each train; such as latest commit date, code freeze date, test phase or dates when the app is submitted to apple the Apple App Store or to Google Play.

Today could be visualized by a movable string. Magic flipcharts (self-adhesive plastic posters) are useful since it is easy to add new ones (and remove old ones) as time goes by.

Guide Board

Capture the working agreement policies from retrospectives by drawing and writing on Post-its. Actually portraying the policy in a drawing makes the policy easier to remember, stirs great discussions and makes the **Guide Board** easier to read for the team. For each, sprint add a new column.

If a policy is poorly followed, push the Post-it down to the "Under Observation" row. In the next retro evaluate your ability to follow the policy, and then either put it back into its place or close it with a blue note.

When a policy becomes replaced or deprecated, put a blue sticker on the policy. The front of the blue Post-it states the sprint during which it became obsolete and the back side of the Post-it describes the reason why it became deprecated.

Daily Check-in ♥

Not everyone has the luxury of working in a co-located team but still depends on colleagues for discussions. You might for example be an agile coach collaborating a lot with other agile coaches and **you want to easily see who else is in the office**.

When you arrive in the morning, you move your avatar to the current day, and when you leave you move it to "Not here". To make the visualization more fun, why not use LEGO?

Christmas Tree

Do you have a pile of boring chores to take care of? Do you have a dung pile of smelly bugs to deal with before you can launch? Is it Christmas time?

Buy yourselves a table sized **Christmas tree**. Head out for shopping over lunch. Disperse. Everyone buys a couple of presents for a few euros each. For instance, it could be a small gift, something silly or some candy. Hang the presents in the tree.

Policy: When you have completed a boring chore or fixed a bug, you are allowed to reward yourself with a present.

Discipline Track Record

When getting started with Kanban, one of the first challenges is to be truly disciplined regarding the WIP Limits so that they aren't exceeded.

An easy way to be transparent and honest about how disciplined you are as a team is to **keep a track record of how often you break any WIP Limit**.

Print (or draw) monthly calendars. By the end of the Daily Stand-up, check if a WIP Limit is exceeded. If it is, make a red fat ugly blob in the calendar. If not, draw a nice green circle.

Dependency Board ♥

When a team discovers that they need something from another team (in order to begin their own work), they add that to the shared **Dependency Board**. "We need <red> before we can start with <yellow>". The notes are connected with a string.

The board is regularly reviewed by the teams, for instance during the Scrum of Scrums. Once a red note has been resolved the connected yellow Post-its is removed as well.

The Dependency Board can help teams to plan, slice features, foresee needed technical collaboration, as well as finding alternative ways of helping each other.

Bonus: How to peel a Post-it

This might appear to be a stupid tip, who would need to learn how to peel a Post-it from a Post-it deck?

Well, quite many people it seems. To avoid curly Post-its that don't hang flat on the wall, lift the Post-it slightly with a firm grip and **pull it down**. Ta da!

If holding the thumb on the side of the deck doesn't work for you (as shown in the lower right corner) try position the left thumb on top of the stack, under the Post-it you are about to pull.

But hey, what if...

Digital planning tools - If you only use digital planning tools such as JIRA and you have a hard time figuring out how to apply these ideas, well that's life. Hopefully you didn't pay for this book. If you did, still no refund though.

Dis-located team - If your team isn't co-located, perhaps you can position a high resolution webcam in front of the wall or send daily pictures to the team members off-site. Or discuss to rearrange the teams so that each team is co-located.

We don't have whiteboards - Try using magic flipcharts. Or, be a rebel and draw directly on your walls. That will probably speed up the requisition of as many whiteboards as you need.

We only have yellow Post-its - Every policy can be changed. Figure out whom to talk to and go and talk to that person. Or go out and buy more colors and reimburse the purchase. Someone once said "Better ask for forgiveness than to ask for permission."

Example index

➔ More information

Here you find links to articles and blogs explaining some of the examples in greater detail.

Concept Cubes (page 94)
http://conceptcubes.com/

Confidence Smileys (page 16)
http://blog.crisp.se/2015/04/01/jimmyjanlen/the-sprint-burndown-is-dead-long-live-confidence-smileys

Daily Goals (page 95)
http://nomad8.com/daily-stand-up-with-a-goal/

Guide Board (page 99)
http://mattischneider.fr/agile/guide-board/

Hourglass Scrum Wall (page 88)
http://www.strongandagile.co.uk/index.php/the-hourglass-scrumban-board/

Improvement Theme (page 63)
http://blog.crisp.se/2013/05/14/jimmyjanlen/improvement-theme-simple-and-practical-toyota-kata

♥ Sources of inspiration

For most of the examples in this book, it's hard for me to pinpoint where I saw it first or what inspired me. But for the examples below there's a clear source of inspiration.

Arrival/Departure Timeline (page 90)
- Yves Hanoulle, http://www.hanoulle.be/

Christmas Tree (page 101)
- Mattias Skarin, Crisp

Stand-ups on time + high score (page 36)
- Kristinn Árni Lár Hróbjartsson, Plain Vanilla/QuizUp

Daily Check-in (page 100)
- Rolf F. Katzenberger, Pragmatic Teams

Daily Goals (page 95)
- Sandy Mamoli, Nomad8

Dependency Board (page 103)
- LEGO (through Henrik Kniberg, Crisp)

Dotting (page 21)
- Team HW Partners, Spotify

Guide Board (page 99)
- Matti Schneider, http://mattischneider.fr

Hourglass Scrum Wall (page 88)
Craig Strong, Pearson

want to learn... (page 91)
Pierre Neis, Upward Consulting

nbox (page 13)
- Team Gaia, Spotify

Kudos Wall (page 49)
- Jurgen Appelo, http://www.jurgenappelo.com

Pair Programming Matrix (page 59)
- Henrique Imbertti, Spotify

Progress Pie (page 38)
- Pétur Jóhannes Óskarsson, Plain Vanilla/QuizUp

Promiscuous Map (page 80)
- Jan Grape, Crisp

Pyramid Backlog (page 78)
- Gunnar Holmsteinn, Plain Vanilla/QuizUp

Race Track (page 83)
- Georg Olafsson, Meniga

Rotating Facilitator's Hat (page 33)
- Guðfinnur Sveinsson, Plain Vanilla/QuizUp

Stress Level Meter (page 62)
- Crisp Office

Team Habits (page 32)
- Fredrik Lindgren, Crisp

Team Members with Hats (page 31)
- Gunnar Holmsteinn, Plain Vanilla/QuizUp

Team Presence Hours (page 75)
- Hans Brattberg, Crisp

Team Time Zone Clocks (page 81)
- Yves Hanoulle, http://www.hanoulle.be/

Time Invested (page 97)
- Mattias Skarin, Crisp

Today's trick (page 86)
- Edward Dahllöf, Valtech

Tube Poll (page 79)
- Mattias Skarin, Crisp

Reading tips

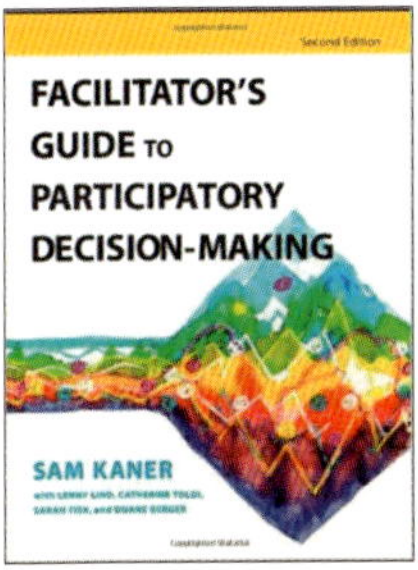

Acknowledgments

Thanks to...

Therése Janlén Ressel – My beautiful wife and partner in crime and adventures who always takes time to give me feedback on things I write and supports me regardless if I occupy our dining table with lego, spends 1 week a month away on Iceland or writes book into the late nights.

Special thanks to my friend and colleague **Hans Brattberg** for encouraging me to publish this book on Google Drive. Turned out the be of awesome value and much fun.

My colleagues at Crisp – For their supportive cheering, generous sharing of ideas, experiences and knowledge, and for relentless and valuable feedback.

All my clients – For allowing me to be a small part of your agile journey and for all the learning opportunities you have offered me. A very special thanks to **Spotify** and **Plain Vanilla**. Spending time with you, learning from you, fighting together with you, and being challenged by you have had a tremendous impact on me. I've grown so much thanks to you.

Acknowledgments (cont)

Big thanks **Yves Hanoulle, Rolf F. Katzenberger** and **Bart Coelus** for great feedback and suggestions through **Google Drive comments**. Many thanks to these online contributors too: **Hafþór Bryndísarson, Edward Dahllöf, Martin Zehle, Erik Buitenhuis, Arlo Belshee**, **Conor Moyne, Pierre Neis, Tobias Modig** and **Tomas Nilsson**.

A special thanks to **Marlowe Klingvall**, who took time to read and give me invaluable feedback on grammar and spelling for every single page.

And finally, thanks to all the **curious anonymous** animals that came by to read the online Google Drive version of this book: Koala, Crow, Ibex, Jackal, Iguana and Kraken. And Rabbit. And Manatee and Cormorant. And Turtle, Panda, Axolotl, Wolf, Sheep and Otter. Oh, I almost forgot; Dingo, Giraffe, Squirrel, Skunk and Bat.

And everyone else I've missed to mention.

Thank you all!

More from Jimmy Janlén

Jennie Discovers!

A small book (24 pages, 10cm x 10cm) about product discovery. Written by Jimmy Janlén and Hans Brattberg.
https://www.crisp.se/crispi1/en

Something Agile Lean Something

Educational posters about everything agile and lean with Lego and Star Wars as a theme.
https://somethingagileleansomething.com

Jimmy Cards

https://www.crisp.se/bocker-och-produkter/jimmy-cards

Concept Cubes

https://conceptcubes.com

Your own examples...

Your own examples...

Your own examples...

Your own examples…